WORDS OF FIRE

IRENE MCCULLUM-HINES

Order this book online at www.trafford.com
or email orders@trafford.com

Most Trafford titles are also available at major online book retailers.

Print information available on the last page.

ISBN: 978-1-4907-8039-9 (sc)
ISBN: 978-1-4907-8038-2 (e)

Trafford rev. 01/24/2017

Trafford
PUBLISHING® www.trafford.com

North America & international
toll-free: 1 888 232 4444 (USA & Canada)
fax: 812 355 4082

A Teenage Crack Mother

I was born in the crack house in the
ghetto to a young teenage mother
Who never knew who her father was?
Who sold her body on the street of the
ghetto corns to get some crack?
She was blinded by crack rock?
The crack mother was at the bottomless pit
of sorrows and lies from the crack rock that
consumed her mind and took away her dreams.
I'm haunted by her nightmares and dreams
and her pain that hurts so bad.
Who loss her life on the crack train.
Who ride the crack train straight to hell?

A Testament of Love

Love is like a fortress protect
You against all trouble
Love can weather every storm
It a building block for
True love
Love can endure hardships
Love is like a warm blanket on
A cold winter's night
Love is like an orchestra if the
Music is in harmony all the instruments
Is working you have created a masterpiece
Of love

Confederate Flag

Say Goodbye to the Confederate Flag!!!
It time say Goodbye to the Confederate Flag.
It is time for the Hatred to stop!
It was Hatred that started the Civil War.
It was Hatred that put us in to slavery.
In it was Hatred that killed the nine People in the Church.
But it is Love that teaches us how to forgive and
it is Love that will teaches us how to grow
And
It is Love that will bring us together.
So say Goodbye to the Confederate Flag
because it is a symbol of Racial Hatred
And
Say Hello to Love.

CRAYON BOX

God came and paint the world
With every color of the crayon box
The world is like the rainbow
So
Beautifully made by God own hand
How wonderful we are made, so beautiful
Like the rainbow colors
I think God for creating the rainbow
Colors
The colors of the crayons box

Underground Railroad

Harriet Tubman made 19 trips to the
South to free the slaves
Under the moonlight
Negros escaping from their masters
Run Negros! Run Negros!
Run! Run! Run!
Follow the North Star running in the dark outdoor bare feet
Dogs are barking and the white men have hunting rifle
Run Negros! Run Negros!
Run! Run! Run!
Run from your slaves master plantation where
the own auction off the runaways slaves after
they beat them and whipping them
Run Negros! Run Negros!
Run! Run! Run!
Under the secret tunnel of Underground Railroad
In the dark of the night

Dedicated To the Memory of Harriet Ross Tubman

EMMETT TILL

❧

Emmett Till was my name the white man killed me
My name is mentioned on black history month
I heard them whisper about Emmett Till.
He
Won't be still his name keep floating
around black history month
Emmett Till won't die
We cannot keep them silence
About Emmett Till story
Around this neck lace with barbed wire
But his story did not die
He keeps coming to life on black history month

Dedication to the memory of Emmett Till

ENSLAVE

America freedom is
Determined on what
Color is your skin and
Your skin color can determine
The costs of freedom
Or
The price of enslave

FLOWER OF LOVE

A
Rose
Is
Like
A
Piece
Of
Art
That
Bloom
In
The
Mornings
Sun
It
Shows
Love
In
The
Heart
And
Beauty
In
The
Eyes
It's
GOD
Blessing
On
High

Freedom Summer

*Mississippians, shame on you for not
wanting your black brothers to vote.
The freedom summer workers were rocked by horror
and shame by the mistreatment of Mississippians
Everyone should have the right to vote in order
to enjoy the laws of the land and to have a
chance to the sweet taste of liberty.
Shame on you Mississippians for not wanting
your black brothers to vote we declare justice
for all people shame on you Mississippians.
Shame! Shame! Shame!*

*I dedicate to the Freedom Summer works
of (1964) that work in Mississippi*

FREEDOM

America is the land of freedom and opportunity,
But we are not completely free.
The promise of freedom held out on hope and
self-determination and Educational.
With no opportunities for a black man
freedom meant an end of a whip
If you are a black man,
how does a man look for freedom for his self
and enslave someone else?
Why is the color Black always the victim
On the racial war for freedom

GOD Speak To Me

The man whispered, "God, speak to me"
Let me know you are real
So the man yelled "God, speak to me"
The man cried out "God, I need your help"
"Touch me, God, and let me know you are real"
"God, let me see you."
Let me touch your hand
Reach for me
And
God, said I was here
All the time
"I woke you up this morning"
I was at bed side
I was by your side all time
I was the one who dry your tear
During the most troublesome time in your life
That time I carried you
I love you my child
I will never leave you
Or
Forsaken You I will always be there

GOD

GOD knows your heart
He is the strength of our
Life
All you have to do
Is obey him trust in him
He will lead you on the path
Of righteousness
Believe in GOD
Because
He is our rock
And
Our salvation

GUILTY

Freddie gray was found guilty of the charge of
being a black man on the ghetto street.
The police beaten him down and they crucifixion
that young black man he die in the police van.
No Justice! No Peace! For Freddie gray!
The six police officers have been suspended but
who will pay for the death of Freddie gray.
Freddie gray neck was broken like his ancestry the
Slave
No Justice! No Peace! For Freddie Gray!

I dedicate in the memory of Freddie Gray

HEROES

Listen to the black people cry about their heroes
That they lost in the battle.
Who fight for them against the racial war?
Gun blasts to Martin Luther King by assassin
Four years for Bobby Seal for helping the black cause.
Them I realize that I am somewhere in
this battle loss in this racial war.
A flash back to Medgar Evers how
they silence him with a gun
But there hatred killed him
Black people are weeping for their
heroes that they lost in battle.
We are going to ride this history
train all the way out to the
Next stop

If you see me Struggle

Everyone says life is easy
But I say living is hard
People struggle all the time
And
Sometime they fall
But you will never see me fall
Because
God got my hand he is going to Carrie
Me though it all
But
If I'm weak or not I'm going to stand tall
I'm going to fight to live
Even though I'm destined to die
I'm going fight to live even though it's hard
And
I may struggle through it all
But
You will never see me fall

The Thirsty of Love

I'm thirsty
For your love
I'm thirsty
For your lips
I'm thirsty for your body
I'm thirsty for your soul
Behind every thirsty soul
There is someone
Who will try to escaped from the thirsty of love
But love will
Keep pull them back in
For the thirsty of love
I'm thirsty I'm thirsty
For your love
The thirsty of love will never
Die!
I'm thirsty for your
Love

JESUS

He is my heart and soul
He is everything to me
He is greater than any rule
Bigger than any king
He call our everlasting father
He call wonderful, counselor
He call the prince of peace
He call king of king and Lord of Lord
He call Emmanuel, He is call I am
He call alpha and omega the beginning and the ending
He is worthy to be praise
Let worship him in the Beauty of holiness

"The gift of GOD is eternal life in Christ Jesus our Lord"
Romans 6:23

Judgment Day

Pray we be ready when that
Great day come when God
Judge his people
Gabriel blow his trumpet
God rain down fire
All nations wake-up to be judge
Gabriel blow his trumpet shakes the hold foundation's
We would see the graves
Burst open
In the twinkling of an eye
We are caught up in the air before God judgment bar
The sinners will be standing on the left
And
The righteous will be standing on the right
When God rain down fire, Gabriel blow his trumpet
God will divide the sheep's from the goats
The ones on the right God is going
to say enter into my kingdom
The ones on the left into hell goodbye to the sinners
When God rain down by fire

LAWS

No universal laws
Was created for the common cause
For the black man loss
Or
For the history of the black man
That
Can erase the black man pain
Nor
Can it break the black man chains?

LET ME FLY

When my final prayer
Is over
I will fly home to meet
My Jesus
I will fly home on Angel wings
I would fly away to heaven
No more tears there
Oh how sweet the harmony
Is
Where there are praising our
Lord
Angels will be blowing sweet spirit wind
High in the sky
So I can fly! So I can fly!
Home to my Jesus on Angel wings
Let me fly.

LET ME LOVE YOU

Let me have your love
Give me your mind
Let me have your heart
Give me your love
Let me romance you
Let me ease all your pain
Let me see that your love is unconditional
Everything I feel for you is visible
Oh how sweet it is
Now every inch of me belongs to you
Let me love you

LORD

Lord be with us,
We are surrounding
With his Love each every day
There is No fear in the Lord
His eye is upon us,
His arms is wraps around us
His ear is open to
Our prayer
His grace is sufficient
His promise unchangeable

Lost

I am Lost in his world
I am Lost in his love
I am Lost, I am lost
I am so lost, I am so lost
I am lost in his words
I am lost in this arm
I am lost in this thing you called love
he toke my heart throw it away
I am lost in this love story
sometimes he take my heart out in play with it
I am so lost in this thing you call love.
I am lost

LOVE

Love Arrives
Love is commitment to each other
Love is laughing
Love ask no questions
Love is for all age
Love is forever
Love strikes away the chains of fear
From our souls
Love is you and me

Maya Angelou she was a beautiful poet she wrote about love pain and wisdom she fought against discrimination. Her poem for life should be this

TO SPEAK THE TRUTH
TO THE PEOPLE

To talk sense to the people
Free them with reason
Free them with honesty
Free the people with Love and Courage and wisdom.
Spare them the fantasy
Of
Fantasize on black hatred
She spoke with a loud voice and people stop to listen
She Speak the truth to the people's
through her poetry
She speaks to free their mind and help to
educate the black minds about black Love.
She Help build a strong black nation through her poetry
She Speak to the mind of the people
She Speak truth

MY FIRST LOVE

First Love Blossoms
Then the touch
Then smile
With the look
With my heart beat fast
My heads on cloud nine
My hands is shake
It true love
It not a dream
If so don't wake me up
No more darkness
No more hatred
No more tears
Oh what a joy this is
To Love someone
With all Your Heart

My Lover

Kiss me again and again for your love is its better than wine
Come and lie beside me and make love to me
You'll love is like perfume I will flourish in it
Your eyes are like's diamonds...
Your lips are like rose petals soft,
come and lie here on the grass
Smell the flowers yes spring is here
and young love is a growing
I see your black beautiful face making sweet love to me.
My lover I will blossom in your love let my hands
touch your Strong black beautiful body,
Wake me in the morning with your love
as the sunrise so wills our love.

NIGGER

We rap about word nigger
Call each of Niggers
We used this word Nigger on ourselves
When it means to be nothing more
But a servant to the slave master
Word Nigger makes us lose
All respect and pride for each of others
We forget those tears that was shared
Because of the word Nigger and yet we still
Use this word Nigger
Those that have died because of the word
Nigger
We were chained dragged through the mud
Call Nigger
How fasts we forget
About the word nigger and about the
Lynch mobs
We were burned and beating then
Sold on A block in chains braces and
Call nigger
Our freedom was taken our black men was
Castrated our black women was rape and
Our black children were sold and we still use this word
Nigger

OH LORD,

Thank You for the gift of LIFE and HOPE
You gave us every day.
Because of You we know
That no problem is too difficult or hard
And even death does not have power over us.
We celebrate Your life, JESUS,
With our hearts full of praise and gratitude Thank You

Dear Lord
For who You are and all You've done for us!
Amen.

OPEN

Open your eyes
Open your heart
Open your mind
Open to love
Open to find
Open to life

POISON AT BIRTH

Racism is still alive
It's bad and it's ugly and
It's crazy.
Racism will never die,
As
Long as we have racial profiling
We will always have discrimination and
Stereotyping,
We will never get past
Skin color because we was
Poison at Birth

POLICE VIOLENCE

There is a War on black men today the police
Will beat you down to the ground
The police hate your skin color
They hate that I'm a black man
So he will kicks my ass
And
Spray me with tear gas
Their No Mercy for a Black man
The police are going to kill you
He is a cold hearted killer
And
You asked me why I hate the cop
Because they
Look at every black man same way
If you are educated or not it does not matter
You are still a nigga
That why hatred is so strong for the cop
Because there's nothing you can do
To stop the cop for hating your skin color
The Cops has all the power to make your life a living hell
And
Do not fight back because they will put you in jail
And
Call it resisting arrest
Or
Shoot you several times
And
If you turn around raise your hands high to the sky
You still will be gun down
If you are a black man

Remembering Nelson Mandela

Remember the struggle for freedom a man of color
Nonviolent struggle hatred without
beautiful and intelligent
Strong black man
Stood tall and stood strong
Spoke of peace and love breaking down the
walls and ringing the bells for freedom
But this giant of a man Nelson Mandela
Even in death his spirit lives on fighting
for freedom and justice
Even today
He stands tall, He stands strong
We will remember the struggle for freedom

Irene McCullum-Hines

Revolution

The revolution! The revolution!
There will be no highlight on the CNN news
The revolution! The revolution!
People will be dying
Children would be cry
There be no picture showing
The revolution! The revolution!
The pig will not know
The revolution! The revolution!
The revolution will not be broadcast by the government
The revolution! The revolution!
The people in the ghetto and the crack house
Will not know
The revolution! The revolution!

STAND YOUR GROUND LAW

Another child dies for
The Stand your Ground
Law
Let's kill another black child
And Say it's the
Stand your Ground
Law
Let's kill another black child
So they can never
Grow up
Let's kill another black child
And Say it's the
Stand your Ground
Law
Let's kill! Let's kill!
Black Children

STRUGGLE IN GHETTO

The black people in the Ghetto is struggling and fighting
To stay alive
It's a war going on right here
In the ghetto
It's a daily struggle to stay alive
Young black Child growing up in poverty
And dies in the street of the ghetto
From a gun blast to the face,
Ghetto Street is like living in hell
With no hope of getting out
Then you are loss in the ghetto
With no dream then you are hopeless and with no education
Then you are loss to the drug man
Next stop is prison.

THE GHETTO HELL

The ghetto is hell It hard to survive in the ghetto.
It hell in the ghetto!!
It's like the drug man's who hunt for his next prey.
Crime is everywhere in the ghetto
Death is the story in the ghetto
A young black man die every day in the ghetto street
Gunned down lay in the streets of the ghetto hell!
Why the junkie is sharing their needles in nod out
In the ghetto hell!!

PAIN OF THE GHETTO

The Ghetto pain is built up on hate, sorrow, hardship,
Is felt by everyone
You can look and see the pain in their faces.
Abandon houses and broken steps and rats
are running around in the alleys.
Dreams are loss and slip through the cracks,
trap down here in the ghetto pain
Locked up in chains and on fire loss in the ghetto pain,
I am locked in the ghetto cage and try to keep
my composer in the pain of the ghetto.
I am tried to survive to make a way out of the ghetto
By selling drugs,
No mercy for the black man on the street of the ghetto.
I feel like a slave caught up in the ghetto pain
with the white man still holding the power
To the ghetto,
We are trap with no exit out of the ghetto pain

THE NEGRO RIVER

The Old black women sits in a rocking chair
tells a story about how the slaves was
sing about old Mississippi Rivers.
That ancient Dustin rivers were the
black slave bodies was dump
If you go down by the Mississippi river
you can hear the slaves singing
Each time the wind blows on the Mississippi
Rivers you here the slaves crying and singing
and weeping at the Mississippi River.
There are trap down by the Mississippi
River still searching for their freedom,
At the Mississippi River

THE STRUGGLE

The white man took my life
But he did not take my spirit
My spirit lives on in every black man in America
Now the fight is on to free every black man
Whoever died by the white man violent hands
Who taught the white man to hate did
it exist before he was born
When did the stop trusting?
When did he stop loving?
Who cause him to stop caring?
What made him lose faith in his Fellow human being?
Was it his dad! It is time for us to solve this problem
Negativity, Jealousy, like of love
The hatred is all over!
Why did the court system fuck me over?
Because I am black, if I screamed out for help fuck me
The black man is wrong if he walked the street after dark
Because, I was a black man I was wrong again for being born
A black man, I was wrong to be who I am a black man
In America the wrong age, the wrong skin color
I wrong for being a black man,
Because of that the white man took my life.
Who in the hell told him he was right.
I dedicate to the memory of Trayvon Martin

TIRED

I'm tired of fighting
                    I'm tired of struggling.
I'm tired of people
                        Not understanding me.
I'm tired of the economy
                            Ups and downs twist.
I'm tired of living from paycheck
                                To next paycheck,
And I'm tired of ass holes who
                        Does not give a damn about
                        other people
And I'm tired of kiss assess
            Tired! Tired!

Until We Meet Again

Mom when they said you were going to die,
I refuse to believe it, it cannot be true
How could I allow myself to ever imagine
Saying goodbye to you
You were more than a mother to me
You were my best friend
You always listen to me
I could call you at any time, day or night
Oh how I miss our special talks, we always had fun together
You taught me how to love unconditionally
and how to believe in myself and trust
And God, you gave all you can give to God and family
I never once stopped thinking about you.
Mom I will never say good bye to you because I could
Never bear the pain of losing you and instead I will say
"I love you mom",
Until we meet again

I dedicate to the memory of Marian Singleton – McCullum

WOMEN OF DESTINY

Rise up Hillary Clinton and claim your destiny a women of God.
God has given you a gift.
Arise in your God given gift for the
world is waiting for your release
Rise up! Rise up!
The glass ceiling is broken and the dream of hope
is real, so rise up and expand your wings and
fly, for this is your finest hour. God is calling
you to come forward and impact the world for
all the women that has come before you.
Rise up! Rise up!
Now take you message to the world to show that
we are all race of one people mixed with all colors.
Arise and become a women of true excellence.
Rise up! Rise up!

Printed in the United States
By Bookmasters